The 1999 session of the Southern Baptist Convention, meeting in Atlanta, Georgia, adopted the following motion addressed to the President of the Convention:

"I move that in your capacity as Southern Baptist Convention chairman, you appoint a blue ribbon committee to review the *Baptist Faith and Message* statement with the responsibility to report and bring any recommendations to this meeting next June in Orlando."

President Paige Patterson appointed the committee as follows: Max Barnett (OK), Steve Gaines (AL), Susie Hawkins (TX), Rudy A. Hernandez (TX), Charles S. Kelley, Jr. (LA), Heather King (IN), Richard D. Land (TN), Fred Luter (LA), R. Albert Mohler, Jr. (KY), T. C. Pinckney (VA), Nelson Price (GA), Adrian Rogers (TN), Roger Spradlin (CA), Simon Tsoi (AZ), Jerry Vines (FL). Adrian Rogers (TN) was appointed chairman.

Your committee thus constituted begs leave to present its report as follows:

Baptists are a people of deep beliefs and cherished doctrines. Throughout our history we have been a confessional people, adopting statements of faith as a witness to our beliefs and a pledge of our faithfulness to the doctrines revealed in Holy Scripture.

Our confessions of faith are rooted in historical precedent, as the church in every age has been called upon to define and defend its beliefs. Each generation of Christians bears the responsibility of guarding the treasury of truth that has been entrusted to us [2 Timothy 1:14]. Facing a new century, Southern Baptists must meet the demands and duties of the present hour.

New challenges to faith appear in every age. A pervasive anti-supernaturalism in the culture was answered by Southern Baptists in 1925, when the *Baptist Faith and Message* was first adopted by this Convention. In 1963, Southern Baptists responded to assaults upon the authority and truthfulness of the Bible by adopting revisions to the *Baptist Faith and Message*. The Convention added an article on "The Family" in 1998, thus answering cultural confusion with the clear teachings of Scripture. Now, faced with a culture hostile to the very notion of truth, this generation of Baptists must claim anew the eternal truths of the Christian faith.

Your committee respects and celebrates the heritage of the *Baptist Faith and Message*, and affirms the decision of the Convention in 1925 to adopt the *New Hampshire Confession of Faith*, "revised at certain points and with some additional articles growing out of certain needs. . . ." We also respect the important contributions of the 1925 and 1963 editions of the *Baptist Faith and Message*.

With the 1963 committee, we have been guided in our work by the 1925 "statement of the historic Baptist conception of the nature and function of confessions of faith in our religious and denominational life. . . ." It is, therefore, quoted in full as a part of this report to the Convention:

(1) That they constitute a consensus of opinion of some Baptist body, large or small, for the general instruction and guidance of our own people and others concerning those articles of the Christian faith which are most surely held among us. They

4

are not intended to add anything to the simple conditions of salvation revealed in the New Testament, viz., repentance toward God and faith in Jesus Christ as Saviour and Lord.

(2) That we do not regard them as complete statements of our faith, having any quality of finality or infallibility. As in the past so in the future, Baptists should hold themselves free to revise their statements of faith as may seem to them wise and expedient at any time.

(3) That any group of Baptists, large or small, have the inherent right to draw up for themselves and publish to the world a confession of their faith whenever they may think it advisable to do so.

(4) That the sole authority for faith and practice among Baptists is the Scriptures of the Old and New Testaments. Confessions are only guides in interpretation, having no authority over the conscience.

(5) That they are statements of religious convictions, drawn from the Scriptures, and are not to be used to hamper freedom of thought or investigation in other realms of life.

Baptists cherish and defend religious liberty, and deny the right of any secular or religious authority to impose a confession of faith upon a church or body of churches. We honor the principles of soul competency and the priesthood of believers, affirming together both our liberty in Christ and our accountability to each other under the Word of God.

Baptist churches, associations, and general bodies have adopted confessions of faith as a witness to the world, and as instruments of doctrinal accountability. We are not embarrassed to state before the world that these are doctrines we hold precious and as essential to the Baptist tradition of faith and practice.

5

As a committee, we have been charged to address the "certain needs" of our own generation. In an age increasingly hostile to Christian truth, our challenge is to express the truth as revealed in Scripture, and to bear witness to Jesus Christ, who is *"the Way, the Truth, and the Life."*

The 1963 committee rightly sought to identify and affirm "certain definite doctrines that Baptists believe, cherish, and with which they have been and are now closely identified." Our living faith is established upon eternal truths. "Thus this generation of Southern Baptists is in historic succession of intent and purpose as it endeavors to state for its time and theological climate those articles of the Christian faith which are most surely held among us."

It is the purpose of this statement of faith and message to set forth certain teachings which we believe.

—Baptist Faith and Message Study Committee
Adrian Rogers, Chairman
Max Barnett
Steve Gaines
Susie Hawkins
Rudy A. Hernandez
Charles S. Kelley, Jr.
Heather King
Richard D. Land
Fred Luter
R. Albert Mohler, Jr.
T. C. Pinckney
Nelson Price
Roger Spradlin
Simon Tsoi
Jerry Vines

I. The Scriptures

The Holy Bible was written by men divinely inspired and is God's revelation of Himself to man. It is a perfect treasure of divine instruction. It has God for its author, salvation for its end, and truth, without any mixture of error, for its matter. Therefore, all Scripture is totally true and trustworthy. It reveals the principles by which God judges us, and therefore is, and will remain to the end of the world, the true center of Christian union, and the supreme standard by which all human conduct, creeds, and religious opinions should be tried. All Scripture is a testimony to Christ, who is Himself the focus of divine revelation.

Exodus 24:4; Deuteronomy 4:1-2; 17:19; Joshua 8:34; Psalms 19:7-10; 119:11,89,105,140; Isaiah 34:16; 40:8; Jeremiah 15:16; 36:1-32; Matthew 5:17-18; 22:29; Luke 21:33; 24:44-46; John 5:39; 16:13-15; 17:17; Acts 2:16ff.; 17:11; Romans 15:4; 16:25-26; 2 Timothy 3:15-17; Hebrews 1:1-2; 4:12; 1 Peter 1:25; 2 Peter 1:19-21.

II. God

There is one and only one living and true God. He is an intelligent, spiritual, and personal Being, the Creator, Redeemer, Preserver, and Ruler of the universe. God is infinite in holiness and all other perfections. God is all powerful and all knowing; and His perfect knowledge extends to all things, past, present, and future, including the future decisions of His free creatures. To Him we owe the highest love, reverence, and obedience. The eternal triune God reveals Himself to us as Father, Son, and Holy Spirit, with distinct personal attributes, but without division of nature, essence, or being.

7

A. God the Father

God as Father reigns with providential care over His universe, His creatures, and the flow of the stream of human history according to the purposes of His grace. He is all powerful, all knowing, all loving, and all wise. God is Father in truth to those who become children of God through faith in Jesus Christ. He is fatherly in His attitude toward all men.

Genesis 1:1; 2:7; Exodus 3:14; 6:2-3; 15:11ff.; 20:1ff.; Leviticus 22:2; Deuteronomy 6:4; 32:6; I Chronicles 29:10; Psalm 19:1-3; Isaiah 43:3,15; 64:8; Jeremiah 10:10; 17:13; Matthew 6:9ff.; 7:11; 23:9; 28:19; Mark 1:9-11; John 4:24; 5:26; 14:6-13; 17:1-8; Acts 1:7; Romans 8:14-15; I Corinthians 8:6; Galatians 4:6; Ephesians 4:6; Colossians 1:15; I Timothy 1:17; Hebrews 11:6; 12:9; I Peter 1:17; I John 5:7.

B. God the Son

Christ is the eternal Son of God. In His incarnation as Jesus Christ He was conceived of the Holy Spirit and born of the virgin Mary. Jesus perfectly revealed and did the will of God, taking upon Himself human nature with its demands and necessities and identifying Himself completely with mankind yet without sin. He honored the divine law by His personal obedience, and in His substitutionary death on the cross He made provision for the redemption of men from sin. He was raised from the dead with a glorified body and appeared to His disciples as the person who was with them before His crucifixion. He ascended into heaven and is now exalted at the right hand of God where He is the One Mediator, fully God, fully man, in whose Person is effected the reconciliation between God and man. He will return in power and glory to judge the world and to consummate His redemptive mission. He now dwells in all believers as the living and ever present Lord.

Genesis 18:1ff.; Psalms 2:7ff.; 110:1ff.; Isaiah 7:14; 53; Matthew 1:18-23; 3:17; 8:29; 11:27; 14:33; 16:16,27; 17:5; 27; 28:1-6,19; Mark 1:1; 3:11; Luke 1:35; 4:41; 22:70; 24:46; John 1:1-18,29; 10:30,38; 11:25-27; 12:44-50; 14:7-11; 16:15-16,28; 17:1-5,21-22; 20:1-20,28; Acts 1:9; 2:22-24; 7:55-56; 9:4-5,20; Romans 1:3-4; 3:23-26; 5:6-21; 8:1-3,34; 10:4; I Corinthians 1:30; 2:2; 8:6; 15:1-8,24-28; 2 Corinthians 5:19-21; 8:9; Galatians 4:4-5; Ephesians 1:20; 3:11; 4:7-10; Philippians 2:5-11; Colossians 1:13-22; 2:9; I Thessalonians 4:14-18; I Timothy 2:5-6; 3:16; Titus 2:13-14; Hebrews 1:1-3; 4:14-15; 7:14-28; 9:12-15,24-28; 12:2; 13:8; I Peter 2:21-25; 3:22; I John 1:7-9; 3:2; 4:14-15; 5:9; 2 John 7-9; Revelation 1:13-16; 5:9-14; 12:10-11; 13:8; 19:16.

C. God the Holy Spirit

The Holy Spirit is the Spirit of God, fully divine. He inspired holy men of old to write the Scriptures. Through illumination He enables men to understand truth. He exalts Christ. He convicts men of sin, of righteousness, and of judgment. He calls men to the Saviour, and effects regeneration. At the moment of regeneration He baptizes every believer into the Body of Christ. He cultivates Christian character, comforts believers, and bestows the spiritual gifts by which they serve God through His church. He seals the believer unto the day of final redemption. His presence in the Christian is the guarantee that God will bring the believer into the fullness of the stature of Christ. He enlightens and empowers the believer and the church in worship, evangelism, and service.

Genesis 1:2; Judges 14:6; Job 26:13; Psalms 51:11; 139:7ff.; Isaiah 61:1-3; Joel 2:28-32; Matthew 1:18; 3:16; 4:1;

12:28-32; 28:19; Mark 1:10,12; Luke 1:35; 4:1,18-19; 11:13; 12:12; 24:49; John 4:24; 14:16-17,26; 15:26; 16:7-14; Acts 1:8; 2:1-4,38; 4:31; 5:3; 6:3; 7:55; 8:17,39; 10:44; 13:2; 15:28; 16:6; 19:1-6; Romans 8:9-11,14-16,26-27; I Corinthians 2:10-14; 3:16; 12:3-11,13; Galatians 4:6; Ephesians 1:13-14; 4:30; 5:18; I Thessalonians 5:19; I Timothy 3:16; 4:1; 2 Timothy 1:14; 3:16; Hebrews 9:8,14; 2 Peter 1:21; I John 4:13; 5:6-7; Revelation 1:10; 22:17.

III. Man

Man is the special creation of God, made in His own image. He created them male and female as the crowning work of His creation. The gift of gender is thus part of the goodness of God's creation. In the beginning man was innocent of sin and was endowed by his Creator with freedom of choice. By his free choice man sinned against God and brought sin into the human race. Through the temptation of Satan man transgressed the command of God, and fell from his original innocence whereby his posterity inherit a nature and an environment inclined toward sin. Therefore, as soon as they are capable of moral action, they become transgressors and are under condemnation. Only the grace of God can bring man into His holy fellowship and enable man to fulfill the creative purpose of God. The sacredness of human personality is evident in that God created man in His own image, and in that Christ died for man; therefore, every person of every race possesses full dignity and is worthy of respect and Christian love.

Genesis 1:26-30; 2:5,7,18-22; 3; 9:6; Psalms 1; 8:3-6; 32:1-5; 51:5; Isaiah 6:5; Jeremiah 17:5; Matthew 16:26; Acts 17:26-31; Romans 1:19-32; 3:10-18,23; 5:6,12,19; 6:6; 7:14-25; 8:14-18,29; I Corinthians 1:21-31; 15:19,21-22; Ephesians 2:1-22; Colossians 1:21-22; 3:9-11.

IV. Salvation

Salvation involves the redemption of the whole man, and is offered freely to all who accept Jesus Christ as Lord and Saviour, who by His own blood obtained eternal redemption for the believer. In its broadest sense salvation includes regeneration, justification, sanctification, and glorification. There is no salvation apart from personal faith in Jesus Christ as Lord.

A. Regeneration, or the new birth, is a work of God's grace whereby believers become new creatures in Christ Jesus. It is a change of heart wrought by the Holy Spirit through conviction of sin, to which the sinner responds in repentance toward God and faith in the Lord Jesus Christ. Repentance and faith are inseparable experiences of grace.

Repentance is a genuine turning from sin toward God. Faith is the acceptance of Jesus Christ and commitment of the entire personality to Him as Lord and Saviour.

B. Justification is God's gracious and full acquittal upon principles of His righteousness of all sinners who repent and believe in Christ. Justification brings the believer unto a relationship of peace and favor with God.

C. Sanctification is the experience, beginning in regeneration, by which the believer is set apart to God's purposes, and is enabled to progress toward moral and spiritual maturity through the presence and power of the Holy Spirit dwelling in him. Growth in grace should continue throughout the regenerate person's life.

D. Glorification is the culmination of salvation and is the final blessed and abiding state of the redeemed.

Genesis 3:15; Exodus 3:14-17; 6:2-8; Matthew 1:21; 4:17; 16:21-26; 27:22-28:6; Luke 1:68-69; 2:28-32; John 1:11-14,29; 3:3-21,36; 5:24; 10:9,28-29; 15:1-16; 17:17; Acts 2:21; 4:12; 15:11; 16:30-31; 17:30-31; 20:32; Romans 1:16-18; 2:4; 3:23-25; 4:3ff.; 5:8-10; 6:1-23; 8:1-18, 29-39; 10:9-10,13; 13:11-14; I Corinthians 1:18,30; 6:19-20; 15:10; 2 Corinthians 5:17-20; Galatians 2:20; 3:13; 5:22-25; 6:15; Ephesians 1:7; 2:8-22; 4:11-16; Philippians 2:12-13; Colossians 1:9-22; 3:1ff.; I Thessalonians 5:23-24; 2 Timothy 1:12; Titus 2:11-14; Hebrews 2:1-3; 5:8-9; 9:24-28; 11:1-12:8,14; James 2:14-26; I Peter 1:2-23; I John 1:6-2:11; Revelation 3:20; 21:1-22:5.

V. God's Purpose of Grace

Election is the gracious purpose of God, according to which He regenerates, justifies, sanctifies, and glorifies sinners. It is consistent with the free agency of man, and comprehends all the means in connection with the end. It is the glorious display of God's sovereign goodness, and is infinitely wise, holy, and unchangeable. It excludes boasting and promotes humility.

All true believers endure to the end. Those whom God has accepted in Christ, and sanctified by His Spirit, will never fall away from the state of grace, but shall persevere to the end. Believers may fall into sin through neglect and temptation, whereby they grieve the Spirit, impair their graces and comforts, and bring reproach on the cause of Christ and temporal judgments on themselves; yet they shall be kept by the power of God through faith unto salvation.

Genesis 12:1-3; Exodus 19:5-8; I Samuel 8:4-7,19-22; Isaiah 5:1-7; Jeremiah 31:31ff.; Matthew 16:18-19; 21:28-45; 24:22,31; 25:34; Luke 1:68-79; 2:29-32; 19:41-44; 24:44-48;

John 1:12-14; 3:16; 5:24; 6:44-45,65; 10:27-29; 15:16; 17:6,12,17-18; Acts 20:32; Romans 5:9-10; 8:28-39; 10:12-15; 11:5-7,26-36; 1 Corinthians 1:1-2; 15:24-28; Ephesians 1:4-23; 2:1-10; 3:1-11; Colossians 1:12-14; 2 Thessalonians 2:13-14; 2 Timothy 1:12; 2:10,19; Hebrews 11:39–12:2; James 1:12; 1 Peter 1:2-5,13; 2:4-10; 1 John 1:7-9; 2:19; 3:2.

VI. The Church

A New Testament church of the Lord Jesus Christ is an autonomous local congregation of baptized believers, associated by covenant in the faith and fellowship of the gospel; observing the two ordinances of Christ, governed by His laws, exercising the gifts, rights, and privileges invested in them by His Word, and seeking to extend the gospel to the ends of the earth. Each congregation operates under the Lordship of Christ through democratic processes. In such a congregation each member is responsible and accountable to Christ as Lord. Its scriptural officers are pastors and deacons. While both men and women are gifted for service in the church, the office of pastor is limited to men as qualified by Scripture.

The New Testament speaks also of the church as the Body of Christ which includes all of the redeemed of all the ages, believers from every tribe, and tongue, and people, and nation.

Matthew 16:15-19; 18:15-20; Acts 2:41-42,47; 5:11-14; 6:3-6; 13:1-3; 14:23,27; 15:1-30; 16:5; 20:28; Romans 1:7; 1 Corinthians 1:2; 3:16; 5:4-5; 7:17; 9:13-14; 12; Ephesians 1:22-23; 2:19-22; 3:8-11,21; 5:22-32; Philippians 1:1; Colossians 1:18; 1 Timothy 2:9-14; 3:1-15; 4:14; Hebrews 11:39-40; 1 Peter 5:1-4; Revelation 2–3; 21:2-3.

VII. Baptism and the Lord's Supper

Christian baptism is the immersion of a believer in water in the name of the Father, the Son, and the Holy Spirit. It is an act of obedience symbolizing the believer's faith in a crucified, buried, and risen Saviour, the believer's death to sin, the burial of the old life, and the resurrection to walk in newness of life in Christ Jesus. It is a testimony to his faith in the final resurrection of the dead. Being a church ordinance, it is prerequisite to the privileges of church membership and to the Lord's Supper.

The Lord's Supper is a symbolic act of obedience whereby members of the church, through partaking of the bread and the fruit of the vine, memorialize the death of the Redeemer and anticipate His second coming.

Matthew 3:13-17; 26:26-30; 28:19-20; Mark 1:9-11; 14:22-26; Luke 3:21-22; 22:19-20; John 3:23; Acts 2:41-42; 8:35-39; 16:30-33; 20:7; Romans 6:3-5; 1 Corinthians 10:16,21; 11:23-29; Colossians 2:12.

VIII. The Lord's Day

The first day of the week is the Lord's Day. It is a Christian institution for regular observance. It commemorates the resurrection of Christ from the dead and should include exercises of worship and spiritual devotion, both public and private. Activities on the Lord's Day should be commensurate with the Christian's conscience under the Lordship of Jesus Christ.

Exodus 20:8-11; Matthew 12:1-12; 28:1ff.; Mark 2:27-28; 16:1-7; Luke 24:1-3,33-36; John 4:21-24; 20:1,19-28; Acts 20:7; Romans 14:5-10; 1 Corinthians 16:1-2; Colossians 2:16; 3:16; Revelation 1:10.

IX. The Kingdom

The Kingdom of God includes both His general sovereignty over the universe and His particular kingship over men who willfully acknowledge Him as King. Particularly the Kingdom is the realm of salvation into which men enter by trustful, childlike commitment to Jesus Christ. Christians ought to pray and to labor that the Kingdom may come and God's will be done on earth. The full consummation of the Kingdom awaits the return of Jesus Christ and the end of this age.

Genesis 1:1; Isaiah 9:6-7; Jeremiah 23:5-6; Matthew 3:2; 4:8-10,23; 12:25-28; 13:1-52; 25:31-46; 26:29; Mark 1:14-15; 9:1; Luke 4:43; 8:1; 9:2; 12:31-32; 17:20-21; 23:42; John 3:3; 18:36; Acts 1:6-7; 17:22-31; Romans 5:17; 8:19; I Corinthians 15:24-28; Colossians 1:13; Hebrews 11:10,16; 12:28; I Peter 2:4-10; 4:13; Revelation 1:6,9; 5:10; 11:15; 21–22.

X. Last Things

God, in His own time and in His own way, will bring the world to its appropriate end. According to His promise, Jesus Christ will return personally and visibly in glory to the earth; the dead will be raised; and Christ will judge all men in righteousness. The unrighteous will be consigned to Hell, the place of everlasting punishment. The righteous in their resurrected and glorified bodies will receive their reward and will dwell forever in Heaven with the Lord.

Isaiah 2:4; 11:9; Matthew 16:27; 18:8-9; 19:28; 24:27,30,36,44; 25:31-46; 26:64; Mark 8:38; 9:43-48; Luke 12:40,48; 16:19-26; 17:22-37; 21:27-28; John 14:1-3; Acts 1:11; 17:31; Romans 14:10; I Corinthians 4:5; 15:24-28, 35-58; 2 Corinthians 5:10; Philippians 3:20-21; Colossians

1:5; 3:4; I Thessalonians 4:14-18; 5:1ff.; 2 Thessalonians 1:7ff.; 2; I Timothy 6:14; 2 Timothy 4:1,8; Titus 2:13; Hebrews 9:27-28; James 5:8; 2 Peter 3:7ff.; I John 2:28; 3:2; Jude 14; Revelation 1:18; 3:11; 20:1–22:13.

XI. Evangelism and Missions

It is the duty and privilege of every follower of Christ and of every church of the Lord Jesus Christ to endeavor to make disciples of all nations. The new birth of man's spirit by God's Holy Spirit means the birth of love for others. Missionary effort on the part of all rests thus upon a spiritual necessity of the regenerate life, and is expressly and repeatedly commanded in the teachings of Christ. The Lord Jesus Christ has commanded the preaching of the gospel to all nations. It is the duty of every child of God to seek constantly to win the lost to Christ by verbal witness undergirded by a Christian lifestyle, and by other methods in harmony with the gospel of Christ.

Genesis 12:1-3; Exodus 19:5-6; Isaiah 6:1-8; Matthew 9:37-38; 10:5-15; 13:18-30,37-43; 16:19; 22:9-10; 24:14; 28:18-20; Luke 10:1-18; 24:46-53; John 14:11-12; 15:7-8,16; 17:15; 20:21; Acts 1:8; 2; 8:26-40; 10:42-48; 13:2-3; Romans 10:13-15; Ephesians 3:1-11; I Thessalonians 1:8; 2 Timothy 4:5; Hebrews 2:1-3; 11:39–12:2; I Peter 2:4-10; Revelation 22:17.

XII. Education

Christianity is the faith of enlightenment and intelligence. In Jesus Christ abide all the treasures of wisdom and knowledge. All sound learning is, therefore, a part of our Christian heritage. The new birth opens all human faculties and creates a thirst for knowledge. Moreover, the cause of education in the Kingdom of Christ is co-ordinate with the causes of

16

missions and general benevolence, and should receive along with these the liberal support of the churches. An adequate system of Christian education is necessary to a complete spiritual program for Christ's people.

In Christian education there should be a proper balance between academic freedom and academic responsibility. Freedom in any orderly relationship of human life is always limited and never absolute. The freedom of a teacher in a Christian school, college, or seminary is limited by the pre-eminence of Jesus Christ, by the authoritative nature of the Scriptures, and by the distinct purpose for which the school exists.

Deuteronomy 4:1,5,9,14; 6:1-10; 31:12-13; Nehemiah 8:1-8; Job 28:28; Psalms 19:7ff.; 119:11; Proverbs 3:13ff.; 4:1-10; 8:1-7,11; 15:14; Ecclesiastes 7:19; Matthew 5:2; 7:24ff.; 28:19-20; Luke 2:40; I Corinthians 1:18-31; Ephesians 4:11-16; Philippians 4:8; Colossians 2:3,8-9; I Timothy 1:3-7; 2 Timothy 2:15; 3:14-17; Hebrews 5:12–6:3; James 1:5; 3:17.

XIII. Stewardship

God is the source of all blessings, temporal and spiritual; all that we have and are we owe to Him. Christians have a spiritual debtorship to the whole world, a holy trusteeship in the gospel, and a binding stewardship in their possessions. They are therefore under obligation to serve Him with their time, talents, and material possessions; and should recognize all these as entrusted to them to use for the glory of God and for helping others. According to the Scriptures, Christians should contribute of their means cheerfully, regularly, systematically, proportionately, and liberally for the advancement of the Redeemer's cause on earth.

Genesis 14:20; Leviticus 27:30-32; Deuteronomy 8:18; Malachi 3:8-12; Matthew 6:1-4,19-21; 19:21; 23:23; 25:14-29; Luke 12:16-21,42; 16:1-13; Acts 2:44-47; 5:1-11; 17:24-25; 20:35; Romans 6:6-22; 12:1-2; 1 Corinthians 4:1-2; 6:19-20; 12; 16:1-4; 2 Corinthians 8–9; 12:15; Philippians 4:10-19; 1 Peter 1:18-19.

XIV. Cooperation

Christ's people should, as occasion requires, organize such associations and conventions as may best secure cooperation for the great objects of the Kingdom of God. Such organizations have no authority over one another or over the churches. They are voluntary and advisory bodies designed to elicit, combine, and direct the energies of our people in the most effective manner. Members of New Testament churches should cooperate with one another in carrying forward the missionary, educational, and benevolent ministries for the extension of Christ's Kingdom. Christian unity in the New Testament sense is spiritual harmony and voluntary cooperation for common ends by various groups of Christ's people. Cooperation is desirable between the various Christian denominations, when the end to be attained is itself justified, and when such cooperation involves no violation of conscience or compromise of loyalty to Christ and His Word as revealed in the New Testament.

Exodus 17:12; 18:17ff.; Judges 7:21; Ezra 1:3-4; 2:68-69; 5:14-15; Nehemiah 4; 8:1-5; Matthew 10:5-15; 20:1-16; 22:1-10; 28:19-20; Mark 2:3; Luke 10:1ff.; Acts 1:13-14; 2:1ff.; 4:31-37; 13:2-3; 15:1-35; 1 Corinthians 1:10-17; 3:5-15; 12; 2 Corinthians 8–9; Galatians 1:6-10; Ephesians 4:1-16; Philippians 1:15-18.

XV. The Christian and the Social Order

All Christians are under obligation to seek to make the will of Christ supreme in our own lives and in human society. Means and methods used for the improvement of society and the establishment of righteousness among men can be truly and permanently helpful only when they are rooted in the regeneration of the individual by the saving grace of God in Jesus Christ. In the spirit of Christ, Christians should oppose racism, every form of greed, selfishness, and vice, and all forms of sexual immorality, including adultery, homosexuality, and pornography. We should work to provide for the orphaned, the needy, the abused, the aged, the helpless, and the sick. We should speak on behalf of the unborn and contend for the sanctity of all human life from conception to natural death. Every Christian should seek to bring industry, government, and society as a whole under the sway of the principles of righteousness, truth, and brotherly love. In order to promote these ends Christians should be ready to work with all men of good will in any good cause, always being careful to act in the spirit of love without compromising their loyalty to Christ and His truth.

Exodus 20:3-17; Leviticus 6:2-5; Deuteronomy 10:12; 27:17; Psalm 101:5; Micah 6:8; Zechariah 8:16; Matthew 5:13-16,43-48; 22:36-40; 25:35; Mark 1:29-34; 2:3ff.; 10:21; Luke 4:18-21; 10:27-37; 20:25; John 15:12; 17:15; Romans 12–14; I Corinthians 5:9-10; 6:1-7; 7:20-24; 10:23–11:1; Galatians 3:26-28; Ephesians 6:5-9; Colossians 3:12-17; I Thessalonians 3:12; Philemon; James 1:27; 2:8.

XVI. Peace and War

It is the duty of Christians to seek peace with all men on principles of righteousness. In accordance with the spirit and teachings of Christ they should do all in their power to put an end to war.

The true remedy for the war spirit is the gospel of our Lord. The supreme need of the world is the acceptance of His teachings in all the affairs of men and nations, and the practical application of His law of love. Christian people throughout the world should pray for the reign of the Prince of Peace.

Isaiah 2:4; Matthew 5:9,38-48; 6:33; 26:52; Luke 22:36,38; Romans 12:18-19; 13:1-7; 14:19; Hebrews 12:14; James 4:1-2.

XVII. Religious Liberty

God alone is Lord of the conscience, and He has left it free from the doctrines and commandments of men which are contrary to His Word or not contained in it. Church and state should be separate. The state owes to every church protection and full freedom in the pursuit of its spiritual ends. In providing for such freedom no ecclesiastical group or denomination should be favored by the state more than others. Civil government being ordained of God, it is the duty of Christians to render loyal obedience thereto in all things not contrary to the revealed will of God. The church should not resort to the civil power to carry on its work. The gospel of Christ contemplates spiritual means alone for the pursuit of its ends. The state has no right to impose penalties for religious opinions of any kind. The state has no right to impose taxes for the support of any form of religion. A free church in a free state is the Christian ideal, and this implies the right of free and unhindered access to God on the part of all men, and the right to form and propagate opinions in the sphere of religion without interference by the civil power.

Genesis 1:27; 2:7; Matthew 6:6-7,24; 16:26; 22:21; John 8:36; Acts 4:19-20; Romans 6:1-2; 13:1-7; Galatians 5:1,13; Philippians 3:20; 1 Timothy 2:1-2; James 4:12; 1 Peter 2:12-17; 3:11-17; 4:12-19.

XVIII. The Family

God has ordained the family as the foundational institution of human society. It is composed of persons related to one another by marriage, blood, or adoption.

Marriage is the uniting of one man and one woman in covenant commitment for a lifetime. It is God's unique gift to reveal the union between Christ and His church and to provide for the man and the woman in marriage the framework for intimate companionship, the channel of sexual expression according to biblical standards, and the means for procreation of the human race.

The husband and wife are of equal worth before God, since both are created in God's image. The marriage relationship models the way God relates to His people. A husband is to love his wife as Christ loved the church. He has the God-given responsibility to provide for, to protect, and to lead his family. A wife is to submit herself graciously to the servant leadership of her husband even as the church willingly submits to the headship of Christ. She, being in the image of God as is her husband and thus equal to him, has the God-given responsibility to respect her husband and to serve as his helper in managing the household and nurturing the next generation.

Children, from the moment of conception, are a blessing and heritage from the Lord. Parents are to demonstrate to their children God's pattern for marriage. Parents are to teach their children spiritual and moral values and to lead them, through consistent lifestyle example and loving discipline, to make choices based on biblical truth. Children are to honor and obey their parents.

Genesis 1:26-28; 2:15-25; 3:1-20; Exodus 20:12; Deuteronomy 6:4-9; Joshua 24:15; 1 Samuel 1:26-28; Psalms 51:5; 78:1-8; 127; 128; 139:13-16; Proverbs 1:8; 5:15-20; 6:20-22; 12:4; 13:24; 14:1; 17:6; 18:22; 22:6,15; 23:13-14; 24:3; 29:15,17; 31:10-31; Ecclesiastes 4:9-12; 9:9; Malachi 2:14-16; Matthew 5:31-32; 18:2-5; 19:3-9; Mark 10:6-12; Romans 1:18-32; 1 Corinthians 7:1-16; Ephesians 5:21-33; 6:1-4; Colossians 3:18-21; 1 Timothy 5:8,14; 2 Timothy 1:3-5; Titus 2:3-5; Hebrews 13:4; 1 Peter 3:1-7.